RICHARD THOMPSON

T E A C H E S

Traditional Guitar — Instrumentals —

Unique Arrangements of Irish, Scottish and English Tunes

PLAYBACK+
Speed • Pitch • Balance • Loop

To access audio visit:
www.halleonard.com/mylibrary

Enter Code
1056-0046-6304-0044

Cover Photo by Matt Condon

Audio Editor: George James

Mastered by: Ted Orr at
Nevessa Productions, Woodstock, NY

ISBN 978-0-7935-6256-5

EXCLUSIVELY DISTRIBUTED BY

HAL•LEONARD®

7777 W. BLUEMOUND RD. P.O. BOX 13819 MILWAUKEE, WI 53213

Visit Hal Leonard Online at **www.halleonard.com**

Visit Homespun Tapes at **www.homespun.com**

Audio instruction makes it easy! Find the section of the lesson you want with the press of a finger; play that segment over and over until you've mastered it; easily skip over parts you've already mastered—no clumsy rewinding or fast-forwarding to find your spot; listen with the best possible audio fidelity; follow along track-by-track with the book.

Table of Contents

This book contains music examples, and all of the instructional audio tracks are labeled with track icons (◆) for the ease of locating the corresponding tracks. The remaining tracks listed here contain detailed explanation and instruction for these songs.

♦ Banish Misfortune

To Coda ⊕

D.S. al Coda
(take repeat)

⊕ *Coda*

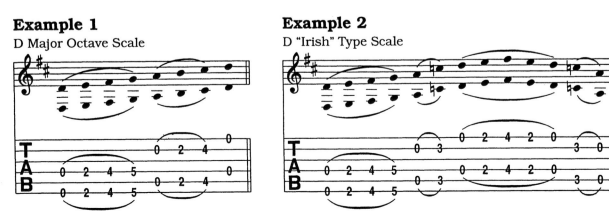

Example 1
D Major Octave Scale

Example 2
D "Irish" Type Scale

◆ McCloud's Reel

"D Modal" Tuning or DADGAD:

①=D ④=D
②=A ⑤=A
③=G ⑥=D

◆11 Maggie Cameron

Tuning:
①=D ④=D
②=C ⑤=G
③=G ⑥=F

Scottish Pipe Tune

8

⬧15⬧ Dargai

Drop D Tuning:
①=E ④=D
②=B ⑤=A
③=G ⑥=D

Slow Bagpipe Tune, Freely

10

11

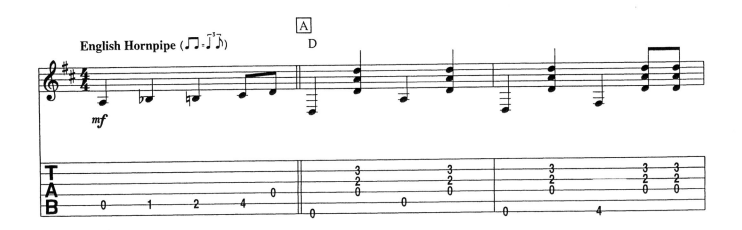 18 The Poppy Leaf Hornpipe
(Accompaniment)

Drop D Tuning:
①=E   ④=D
②=B   ⑤=A
③=G   ⑥=D

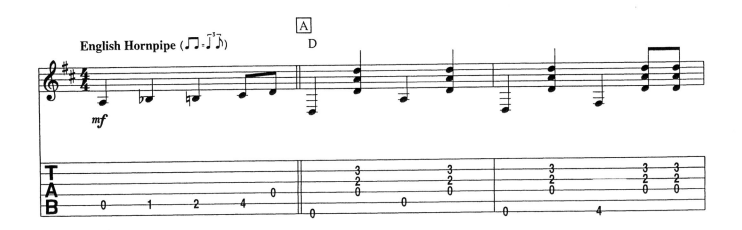

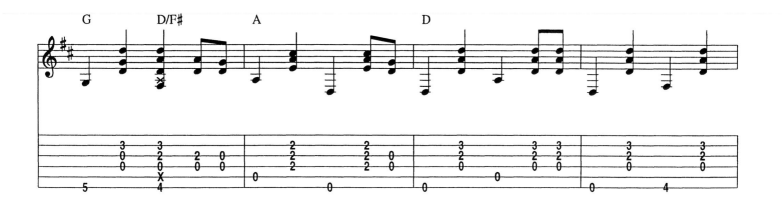

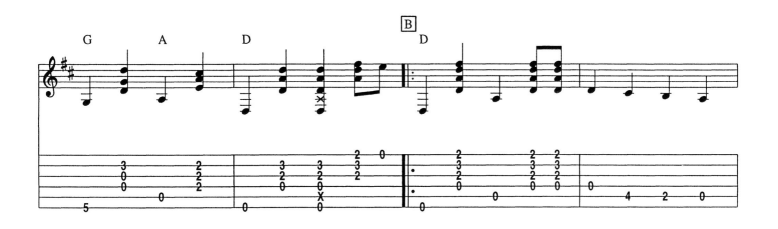

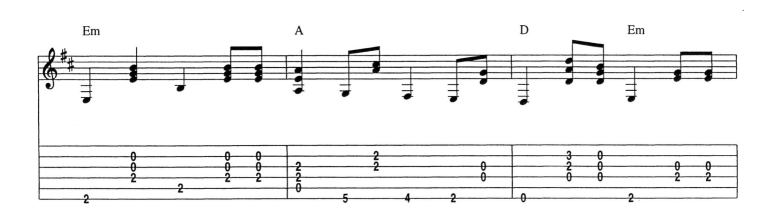

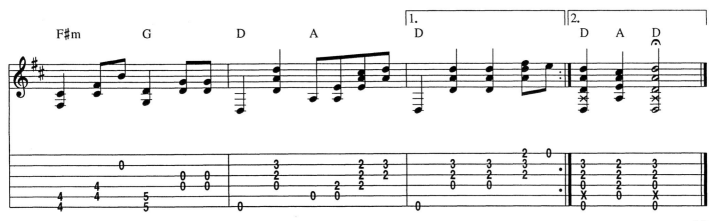

◆21 The Poppy Leaf Hornpipe

Drop D Tuning:
①=E ④=D
②=B ⑤=A
③=G ⑥=D

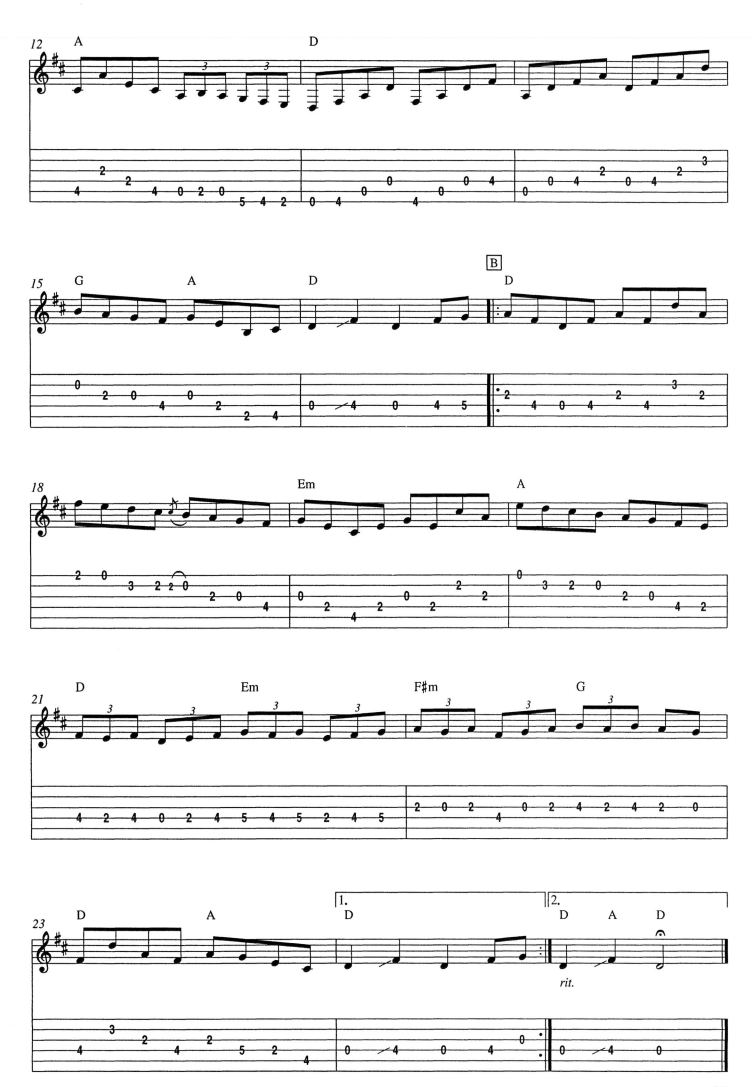

◆22 Variations

Example 1
Insert at measures 1, 5, 9 & 13

Example 2
Insert at measure 17

Example 3
Insert at measure 21, 2nd time

◆24 Rakish Paddy

Drop D Tuning:
①=E ④=D
②=B ⑤=A
③=G ⑥=D

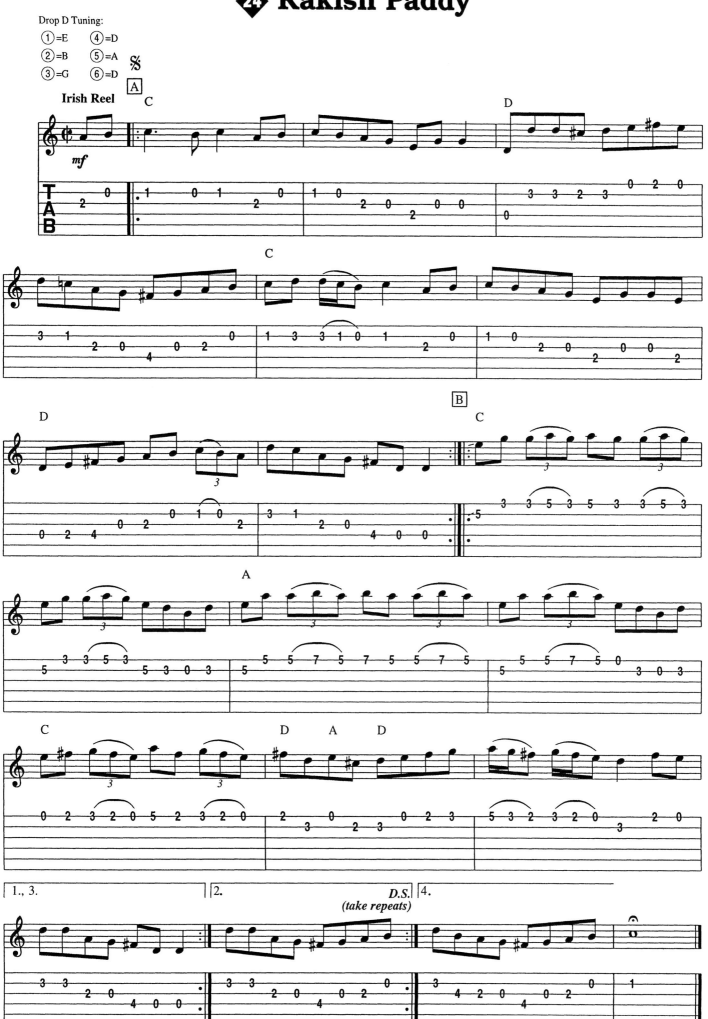

Jenny Lind Polka

Drop D Tuning:
①=E ④=D
②=B ⑤=A
③=G ⑥=D

Polka [A]

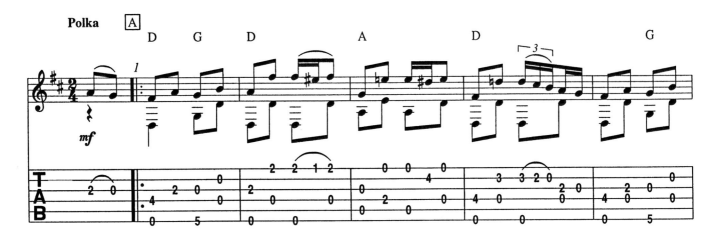

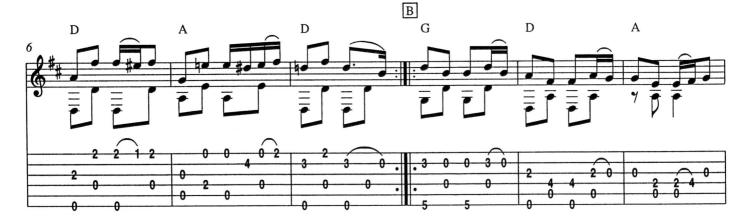

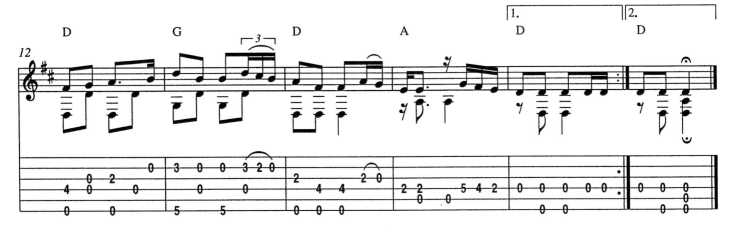

Variations

Example 1
Insert at measure 12

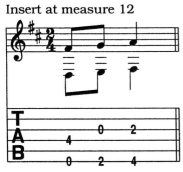

Example 2
Insert at measure 12

Example 3
Insert at measure 12

◆30 ◆ Strathspey

Drop D Tuning, Capo V:
①=E ④=D
②=B ⑤=A
③=G ⑥=D

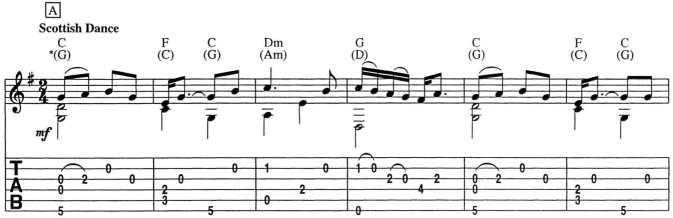

*Symbols in parentheses represent chord names respective to capoed guitar.
Symbols above reflect actual sounding chord. Capoed fret is "0" in TAB.

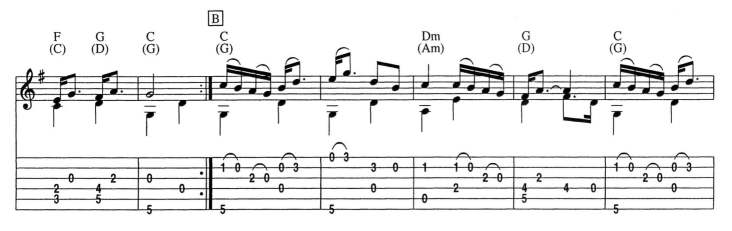

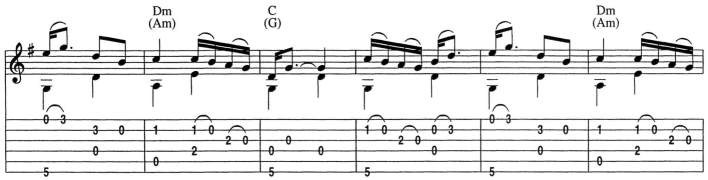

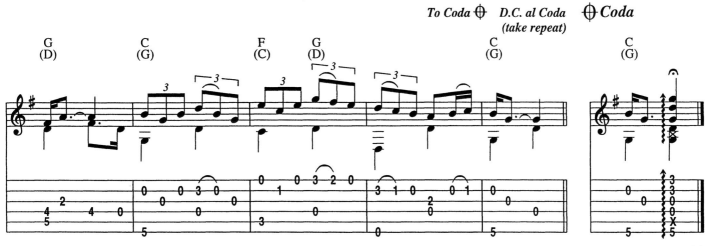

Biography

Named by *Rolling Stone Magazine* as one of the Top 20 Guitarists of All Time, Richard Thompson is also one of the world's most critically acclaimed and prolific songwriters. He has received Lifetime Achievement Awards for Songwriting on both sides of the Atlantic and, in 2011, he received an OBE (Order of the British Empire) personally bestowed upon him by Queen Elizabeth II at Buckingham Palace. In the USA, Thompson has been nominated at the Americana Awards for both "Artist of the Year" and "Song of the Year."

Having co-founded the groundbreaking group Fairport Convention as a teenager in the '60s, Richard Thompson and his mates virtually invented British Folk Rock. He left Fairport to pursue a solo career and a decade-long musical partnership with his then-wife Linda. For the past 30 years he has been a highly successful solo artist, touring globally both as a solo acoustic act and with his electric trio.

A wide range of musicians have recorded Thompson's songs, including Robert Plant, Elvis Costello, REM, Del McCoury, Bonnie Raitt, Patty Lovelace, Los Lobos, Tom Jones, David Byrne, Don Henley, Robert Earl Keen and many others. His massive body of work includes over 40 albums, numerous Grammy nominations, and film soundtracks, including Werner Hertzog's "Grizzly Man."

Thompson's genre defying mastery of both acoustic and electric guitar, along with dizzying energy and onstage wit, continues to earn Richard Thompson massive new fans and a place as one of the most distinctive virtuosos in Folk Rock history.

A Selected Discography

The listing below gives you an overview of this master's recorded works through the years. In addition to these albums there are several "Best of...." compilations, live concert and radio recordings, and other resources by which to hear his wide-ranging and excellent music.

Solo

2015 - *Still*

2014 - *Thompson Family*

2014 - *Acoustic Classics*

2013 - *Electric*

2012 - *Cabaret of Souls*

2012 - *Shoot Out the Lights*
(Expanded and Remastered)

2011 - *Live at the BBC*

2010 - *Dream Attic*

2009 - *Walking On a Wire* (4 Discs)

2009 - *Live Warrior*

2007 - *Sweet Warrior*

2006 - *1000 Years of Popular Music*

2005 - *Grizzly Man Soundtrack*

2005 - *Front Parlor Ballads*

2004 - *Faithless*

2003 - *The Old Kit Bag*

2002 - *Semi-Detached Mock Tudor*

2001 - *Action Packed*

2000 - *The Best of the Island
Record Years*

1991 - *Rumour and Sigh*

1988 - *Amnesia*

1986 - *Daring Adventures*

1985 - *Across a Crowded Room*

1984 - *Small Town Romance*

1983 - *Hand of Kindness*

1981 - *Strict Tempo*

With Linda Thompson

1982 - *Shoot Out the Lights*

1979 - *Sunnyvista*

1978 - *First Light*

1975 - *Pour Down Like Silver*

1975 - *Hokey Pokey*

1974 - *I Want to See the Bright
Lights Tonight*

With Fairport Convention

1970 - *Full House*

1969 - *Liege and Leaf*

1969 - *Unhalfbricking*

1969 - *What We Did on Our Holidays*

1968 - *Fairport Convention*

GUITAR NOTATION LEGEND

Guitar music can be notated three different ways: on a *musical staff*, in *tablature*, and in *rhythm slashes*.

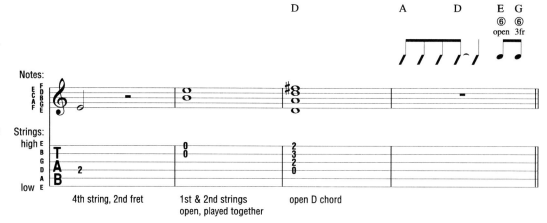

RHYTHM SLASHES are written above the staff. Strum chords in the rhythm indicated. Use the chord diagrams found at the top of the first page of the transcription for the appropriate chord voicings. Round noteheads indicate single notes.

THE MUSICAL STAFF shows pitches and rhythms and is divided by bar lines into measures. Pitches are named after the first seven letters of the alphabet.

TABLATURE graphically represents the guitar fingerboard. Each horizontal line represents a string, and each number represents a fret.

4th string, 2nd fret

1st & 2nd strings open, played together

open D chord

Definitions for Special Guitar Notation

HALF-STEP BEND: Strike the note and bend up 1/2 step.

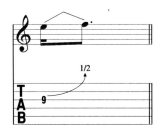

BEND AND RELEASE: Strike the note and bend up as indicated, then release back to the original note. Only the first note is struck.

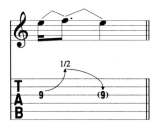

VIBRATO: The string is vibrated by rapidly bending and releasing the note with the fretting hand.

LEGATO SLIDE: Strike the first note and then slide the same fret-hand finger up or down to the second note. The second note is not struck.

WHOLE-STEP BEND: Strike the note and bend up one step.

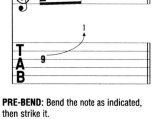

PRE-BEND: Bend the note as indicated, then strike it.

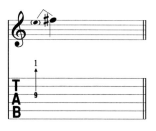

WIDE VIBRATO: The pitch is varied to a greater degree by vibrating with the fretting hand.

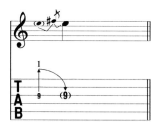

SHIFT SLIDE: Same as legato slide, except the second note is struck.

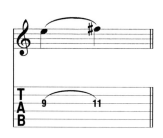

GRACE NOTE BEND: Strike the note and immediately bend up as indicated.

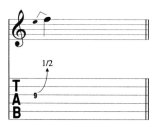

PRE-BEND AND RELEASE: Bend the note as indicated. Strike it and release the bend back to the original note.

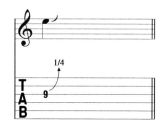

HAMMER-ON: Strike the first (lower) note with one finger, then sound the higher note (on the same string) with another finger by fretting it without picking.

TRILL: Very rapidly alternate between the notes indicated by continuously hammering on and pulling off.

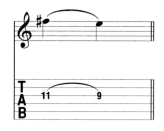

SLIGHT (MICROTONE) BEND: Strike the note and bend up 1/4 step.

UNISON BEND: Strike the two notes simultaneously and bend the lower note up to the pitch of the higher.

PULL-OFF: Place both fingers on the notes to be sounded. Strike the first note and without picking, pull the finger off to sound the second (lower) note.

TAPPING: Hammer ("tap") the fret indicated with the pick-hand index or middle finger and pull off to the note fretted by the fret hand.

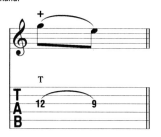

NATURAL HARMONIC: Strike the note while the fret-hand lightly touches the string directly over the fret indicated.

Harm.

PINCH HARMONIC: The note is fretted normally and a harmonic is produced by adding the edge of the thumb or the tip of the index finger of the pick hand to the normal pick attack.

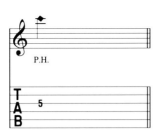

P.H.

HARP HARMONIC: The note is fretted normally and a harmonic is produced by gently resting the pick hand's index finger directly above the indicated fret (in parentheses) while the pick hand's thumb or pick assists by plucking the appropriate string.

H.H.

PICK SCRAPE: The edge of the pick is rubbed down (or up) the string, producing a scratchy sound.

P.S.

MUFFLED STRINGS: A percussive sound is produced by laying the fret hand across the string(s) without depressing, and striking them with the pick hand.

PALM MUTING: The note is partially muted by the pick hand lightly touching the string(s) just before the bridge.

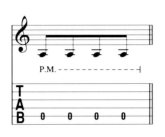

P.M.

RAKE: Drag the pick across the strings indicated with a single motion.

rake

TREMOLO PICKING: The note is picked as rapidly and continuously as possible.

ARPEGGIATE: Play the notes of the chord indicated by quickly rolling them from bottom to top.

VIBRATO BAR DIVE AND RETURN: The pitch of the note or chord is dropped a specified number of steps (in rhythm), then returned to the original pitch.

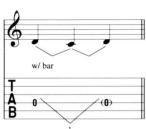

w/ bar

VIBRATO BAR SCOOP: Depress the bar just before striking the note, then quickly release the bar.

w/ bar

VIBRATO BAR DIP: Strike the note and then immediately drop a specified number of steps, then release back to the original pitch.

w/ bar

Additional Musical Definitions

(accent)

- Accentuate note (play it louder).

(accent)

- Accentuate note with great intensity.

(staccato)

- Play the note short.

- Downstroke

∨

- Upstroke

D.S. al Coda

- Go back to the sign (𝄋), then play until the measure marked "*To Coda*," then skip to the section labelled "**Coda**."

D.C. al Fine

- Go back to the beginning of the song and play until the measure marked "*Fine*" (end).

Rhy. Fig.

- Label used to recall a recurring accompaniment pattern (usually chordal).

Riff

- Label used to recall composed, melodic lines (usually single notes) which recur.

Fill

- Label used to identify a brief melodic figure which is to be inserted into the arrangement.

Rhy. Fill

- A chordal version of a Fill.

tacet

- Instrument is silent (drops out).

- Repeat measures between signs.

- When a repeated section has different endings, play the first ending only the first time and the second ending only the second time.

NOTE: Tablature numbers in parentheses mean:
  1. The note is being sustained over a system (note in standard notation is tied), or
  2. The note is sustained, but a new articulation (such as a hammer-on, pull-off, slide or vibrato) begins, or
  3. The note is a barely audible "ghost" note (note in standard notation is also in parentheses).

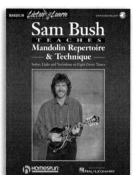

SAM BUSH TEACHES MANDOLIN REPERTOIRE & TECHNIQUE

One of the most versatile and powerful musicians playing today teaches 8 great repertoire tunes that will help mandolin players develop their style and technique. This lesson covers traditional bluegrass tunes as well as jazz-flavored "new-grass" originals: Cotton Patch Rag • Tom & Jerry • Leather Britches • Lime Rock • Banjalin • Diadem • Norman and Nancy • and Russian Rag.

00695339 Book/Online Audio.....................$19.99

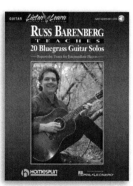

RUSS BARENBERG TEACHES 20 BLUEGRASS GUITAR SOLOS

REPERTOIRE TUNES FOR INTERMEDIATE PLAYERS
One of America's top bluegrass guitarists teaches a variety of flatpicking solos for twenty favorite songs and instrumentals. Played slowed-down and up-to-speed for learning players, with rhythm tracks availble for download or streaming online for great practice sessions. Songs: Liberty • Soldier's Joy • Forked Deer • Eighth of January • Hot Corn, Cold Corn • Down Yonder • John Henry • Blackberry Blossom • Leather Britches • and more. Level 3

00695220 Book/Online Audio...$19.99

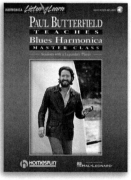

PAUL BUTTERFIELD – BLUES HARMONICA MASTER CLASS

Paul Butterfield was an original and groundbreaking blues harmonica player who brought acoustic Delta blues playing into the electrified blues/rock scene pioneered by Muddy Waters, Little Walter and others. In this rare instructional book with online audio instruction, he teaches many of the techniques that made him famous: note- bending, tongue-blocking and tremolo, as well as many great blues licks and tricks.

00699089 Book/Online Audio.....................$19.95

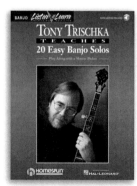

TONY TRISCHKA EASY BANJO SOLOS

Strengthen your skills while building a repertoire of great bluegrass banjo pieces! Tony Trischka has personally chosen twenty traditional banjo solos that will teach you new ideas and add to your arsenal of licks and techniques. On the online audio, Tony performs each tune slowly, then up to speed, providing invaluable tips and explanations as he goes. By the time you have mastered all of these solos, you'll have acquired the basic skills necessary to play in the styles of Earl Scruggs, Don Reno, Sonny Osborne, and other bluegrass greats.

00699056 Book/Online Audio...$19.95

STEVE KAUFMAN'S FOUR-HOUR BLUEGRASS WORKOUT

with Bennie Boling (banjo)
Here's a great way to improve your picking, build up speed and stamina, and get those licks and solos working – no matter what instrument you play! Whether you are a professional or a "parking lot" player, these fabulous sessions will get your fingers in shape – fast! On the four CDs, you have a dedicated bluegrass band playing rhythm to give you solid back-up to 49 great tunes, both slowed-down and up-to-speed. Steve plays the lead parts so you can learn to solo with a band.

00641379 Book/CD Pack...$44.95

TONY TRISCHKA – BANJO BUNDLE PACK

Tony Trischka Teaches 20 Easy Banjo Solos (00699056) and the DVD *Classic Bluegrass Banjo Solos* (00641567) in one money-saving pack. You'll get hours of in-depth banjo instruction from one of the world's best players and teachers, and will learn the licks, solos and techniques of the great historical pickers: Scruggs, Stanley, Reno, et al.

00642060 Book/CD/DVD Pack....................$44.95

ALL STAR BLUEGRASS JAM ALONG

BACKUPS, LEAD PARTS AND NOTE-FOR-NOTE TRANSCRIPTIONS FOR 21 ESSENTIAL TUNES
featuring Todd Phillips
Book/CD Packs
These fabulous collections for players of all levels feature 21 must-know bluegrss songs & instrumentals, created especially for learning players by the genre's leading artists. The artist plays a basic solo that states the melody of the tune, then a more adventurous improvisation, and each solo is transcribed in detail. The CD provides the audio versions of the solos, plus multiple rhythm tracks performed at moderate tempo for easy play-along. This great series will help you build your repertoire & get your licks in shape, so you can shine in your next performance or jam session! Songs include: Bill Cheatham • Blackberry Blossom • Down in the Willow Garden • I Am a Pilgrim • I'll Fly Away • In the Pines • John Hardy • Old Joe Clark • Soldier's Joy • more!

00641947	Bass	$19.95
00641943	Guitar	$19.95
00641946	Fiddle	$19.95
00641945	Mandolin	$19.95
00641944	Banjo	$19.95

Prices, contents and availability subject to change without notice.